MW00414166

LET'S TALK ABOUT
AIDS
AND
SEX

RODNEY GAGE

BROADMAN PRESS
NASHVILLE, TENNESSEE

*This book is dedicated
to those to whom I love
to speak the most—
America's teenagers.*

Contents

Acknowledgments

WHEN YOU HAVE AN IDEA, you often need someone standing behind you, constantly motivating and inspiring you, to put that idea into action. For me, that someone is my father. I wouldn't be where I am today if not for my father, Freddie Gage, who always challenges me to be my best.

Many thanks to Kaye Moreno, whose writing expertise, creativity, and perseverance helped me make my vision become a reality. Thanks to Ruben Rendon for creating the art design for the book cover. Also, thanks to Sandy Ballard for her creative and skillful ability to format this text.

My gratitude and appreciation go also to Robert McGee, Don Sapaugh, and all the people at Rapha Treatment Centers for their thoughts and suggestions. Their help will never be forgotten.

Of course, there is no way I can forget to thank the person I love most, my wife Michelle. Her Christlike example challenges me every day to be more like Jesus. She never grows tired of my constant requests for her opinion. Thank you, Michelle, for being my best friend and for always being there when I need you. I love you.

Foreword

T HE AIDS TRAGEDY now affects us all. No one can miss either its intensity or immensity. In almost every morning paper I read something new about the problem: the theories of its origin in Africa, how a family is coping with the father's debilitating disease, a new treatment concept, another famous person who has died, a more emphatic statistic about its spread. Some people cry out for individual attention; some demand governmental intervention; some just want the threat to go away.

The inevitable questions are asked: "Why?" "How?" "When?" Scientists and doctors have been unable to accurately determine the origin of the virus which causes AIDS. No one knows why the plague has attacked our world: God's judgment, perhaps, or simply another example of creation's fallenness. But its rapid spread is clearly due to sexual hyperactivity.

Perhaps we should look beyond the question, "Why AIDS?" and ask instead, "Why do people have such a blatant disregard for the obvious hazards of sexual promiscuity?" Originally, homosexual activity was identified as the primary culprit of the spread of AIDS. Today, we must add prostitution, as well as bisexual and heterosexual promiscuity, as petri dishes which breed the dreaded plague. Even though images of pain, fear, and death are repeated throughout the media, something propels people to keep taking the sexual risks inherent in the spread of AIDS.

People crave intimacy. They want to belong. They want to feel close and connected to someone else. In addition, many of them also want to "act out" against an uncontrolled person or event that causes deep emotional wounds in their lives. The powerful combination of rebellion against one person and craving for love from another drives many people to take foolish risks. They hope they will get what they really want and need . . . but momentary passion usually turns into prolonged emptiness. And far too often the possibility of contracting HIV becomes a reality.

Young people, especially, need to sort out their deep and complex drives for love and self-worth. They need to establish a strong identity so they can make good choices about relationships. Rodney Gage has helped tens of thousands of young people fill their craving for love with the love of Christ. Beneath the medical complications of HIV lies a spiritual issue. Rodney exposes the roots of the problem so people can grasp the deep spiritual motivations and fulfillments available to them. Only then will they have the capacity and the will to make good and godly choices.

This book will help you understand the issues of HIV and AIDS, but more than that, it will reveal underlying needs, hopes, and desires which God has promised He can meet. Rodney offers hope, help, and genuine insight into the tragic AIDS epidemic.

ROBERT S. MCGEE
PRESIDENT AND FOUNDER OF RAPHA

RAPHA, a nationally recognized health care organization, provides in-hospital care with a Christ-centered perspective for adults and adolescents suffering with psychiatric and substance abuse problems. The truths presented in *The Search for Significance* (written by Robert S. McGee, Founder and President of Rapha) form the foundational cornerstones that provide the balance of spiritual and clinical therapy in the Rapha Treatment Centers program.

For additional information about Rapha, call 1 (800) 383–HOPE.

The Search for Significance, Codependency: A Christian Perspective, and *Rapha's 12-Step Program to Overcoming Codependency* are only a few of the books available at **RAPHA RESOURCES**.

Small group resources are also offered for a wide range of topics such as marriage, family and work life, parenting, self-esteem, co-dependency, stress, anxiety, grief, divorce recovery, chemical dependency, eating disorders, sexual addiction, and sexual abuse.

To obtain a free catalog of books, audio and video tapes, and small group resources, call 1 (800) 562–1250.

Introduction

MEDIA REPORTS CONCERNING the AIDS epidemic sometimes seem over-whelming. For example, a recent Gallup Poll states: "Since the announcement from Magic Johnson about having contracted HIV, he has now become more popular among young people than the President of the United States, George Bush."

F. Scott Fitzgerald once wrote: "Show me a hero, and I'll show you a tragedy." He might have written: "Show me *anyone*, and I'll show you a tragedy." You don't have to be a hero—there are tragedies in all our lives.

Never before have we been faced with an epidemic like AIDS, which has the potential to wipe out an entire society. According to medical experts, millions of people are already suffering. Some are innocent victims, but most are paying the ultimate price for sexual sin.

During the past five years, God has allowed me to speak to over one million young people in public and private schools across the nation. I often wish that parents could travel with me for just one week to hear what I hear and see what I see in the faces of hurting youth who are searching for the answers to life.

Today's generation of young people has a distorted view of what love and sex are all about. Because of the inconsistencies in so many homes—the absence of love, attention, and affection from parents—young people are being taught from other sources that it's acceptable, as rock singer Madonna puts it, to "express yourself."

Our younger generation is getting the message that having sex is the thing to do, as long as it's "safe sex." There is no doubt that teens are having sex—the question is, is it safe?

In this book, I will give what I believe to be the ultimate answer to this controversial question. I have heard hundreds of stories from young people who are scarred and hurting from previous sexual experiences. To them, I will offer forgiveness, hope, and a new beginning in Jesus Christ. And to those who have not yet become sexually active but may be considering it, I want to present some facts and suggestions that they should consider before acting on their impulses.

I have asked God to help me communicate in an honest, yet simple, way how young people can have a sense of worth and self-respect through sexual purity. I believe He has done that.

RODNEY GAGE

1

> *"I'm telling kids—no sex is the safest sex."*
>
> Earvin "Magic" Johnson
> Former member, L.A. Lakers

Living and Dying in the Age of AIDS

"**M**Y LIFE HAS BEEN sheer hell. . . . AIDS has slowly destroyed me. . . . Can you imagine what it's like to realize you're losing weight in your fingers and that your body may be using its muscles to try to survive? Or do you know what it's like to look at yourself in a full-length mirror before you shower—and you only see a skeleton? Do you know what I did? I slid to the floor and I cried."

From that point on, Kimberly Bergalis put a blanket over the mirror before taking a shower. She was one of five patients who, in 1987, accidentally contracted AIDS during a procedure by her dentist. Bergalis died at age 23 of AIDS-related tuberculosis that destroyed her body and her brain.

Among other horrifying symptoms, she lost over 40 pounds, had her hair fall out, and suffered from nausea, vomiting, diarrhea, night sweats, and chronic fevers of 103 to 104 degrees. And a fungus-like white fur eventually coated the inside of her mouth, throat, gums, and lips.[1]

A HIGH PRICE FOR PASSION? _____

As of February, 1992, Americans who had contracted AIDS (Acquired Immune Deficiency Syndrome) numbered 206,000. Even worse, as many as one million others may now be infected with HIV, the virus that causes AIDS, but are not yet suffering from the disease. Nearly 46,000 were infected in 1991 alone. An estimated 140,000 AIDS victims have died.[2]

Cable Network News (CNN) reports that one out of every 100 men and one of every 800 women are infected with the HIV. Every 13 minutes, someone, somewhere, contracts HIV.

In 1986, stunned health workers warned that the disease might eventually claim more lives than either the Korean or Vietnam wars. The current AIDS death toll (about 140,000) is more than that of the two wars *combined*—and more people are expected to die of AIDS during the next two years than have died in the last ten.[3]

The phenomenal spread of AIDS in the U.S. and other parts of the world might be best illustrated by the following story told by Moody Adams on his audio tape, "Aids: You Just Think You're Safe."

One night a man—bored with television and the monotony of his routine as a husband and father—went looking for excitement. It was easier than he thought to create an excuse to be gone for the night, and then he headed for a popular local nightspot.

Seeing a beautiful young woman sitting alone at the bar, he walked over and sat down. She was welcoming and seductive, and she flirted outrageously. *What harm could possibly come from a little innocent flirtation?* he asked himself.

The man introduced himself, and, as the evening wore on, one drink turned into several. He liked her more and more—he liked the way she looked, the way she laughed, the way she listened to him, and especially the way she leaned over occasionally to touch him.

She was undoubtedly the sexiest woman he'd seen in a long time, and he didn't want the night to end. He asked her to leave with him, and she readily agreed. After checking into a nearby motel, they had uninhibited sex until their passion was spent and both were exhausted.

The next morning the man woke slowly, remembering where he was and what had happened in the darkness of the night. He rolled over, expecting to find his beautiful partner next to him. But the bed was empty, except for the lingering scent of perfume. As he rose to go into the bathroom to shower, he thought, *She was one classy lady, and though I may never see her again, this was one night I'll never forget.*

Something caught his eye as he walked through the bathroom door—something bright and colorful. His smile faded as he stared in shock at the words written on the mirror—in the same shade of red lipstick he had kissed from her lips the night before.

His lady's parting message: "WEL-COME TO THE WONDERFUL WORLD OF AIDS."[4]

Though the words were cruelly shocking, they were painfully accurate. Today we live during an age in which our world is confronted by the deadliest of diseases—one for which there is no cure—AIDS.

These days, if you decide to have sex with someone, you are not just at risk of contracting AIDS from that person. You also risk exposure to the HIV from every partner that person has ever had, with every partner each of those partners ever had, and so on and so on. The list could be endless.

AIDS: SOMEONE ELSE'S DISEASE?

There's another story that almost everyone around the world has heard by now, about a man who had many sexual partners. The man was regarded as a hero, a role model for thousands of young people. He was on top of the world. He seemed to have a magic touch, in the sense that he was incredibly successful at everything he did—and he made it look so easy.

Once a skinny kid from a black Michigan neighborhood, he rose to the pinnacle of success, making millions of dollars each year. His "magic" athletic ability had made him one of the most prominent sports figures of the 1980s.

Kids idolized him and adults were dazzled by his charisma. It didn't matter to his millions of fans whether they had ever been close enough to give him a high five, ask for his autograph, or even see him perform in person. They felt as if they knew him.

But no amount of hero worship or magic could change what the doctors told 32-year-old Earvin "Magic" Johnson on the evening of October 25, 1991. The guard for the Los Angeles Lakers for twelve record-breaking years had tested positive for HIV, the virus which causes AIDS.

Two weeks later, on November 7, the soft-spoken giant stood at the Great Western Forum, the home of the Lakers and site of many of his great moments in basketball. As the cameras whirred and clicked and flashed, he announced his retirement from professional basketball, a decision which shocked and saddened the nation. The magic that had followed him throughout a phenomenal career seemed to have deserted him.

Never mind that he had shocked the world—Magic had shocked himself. Johnson admitted that he was like many other Americans—totally ignorant of the deadly reality of AIDS.

"To me, AIDS was someone else's disease," he said. "It was a disease for gays and drug users, not for someone like me. Now I know my ignorance could cost me my life."[5]

Sadly enough, that same ignorance affects thousands of Americans today. Perhaps you are one of the many with an "It can't happen to me" attitude. I hope not, but if so, the information in this book is for you.

Medical experts are quick to admit they don't know everything there is to know about AIDS. It seems new information is discovered almost daily. But one fact has been clear since the disease was identified in the early 1980s— *there is no cure.* AIDS is a real and growing epidemic, one that is almost certain to touch someone you know.

HOW AIDS HAS SPREAD _____

The AIDS epidemic hit the U.S. in three "waves." The first wave, which occurred among homosexual men, is now thought to be leveling off. The second wave is spreading through intravenous drug users, and has yet to reach its peak. The third wave, still in its initial phases, is being spread by heterosexuals— both men and women.

Magic Johnson said he contracted HIV by having unprotected sex with a woman who had the virus—but he doesn't know who, where, or when. He openly admitted his involvement with many women during his travels with the Lakers. In his own words, he was "never at a loss for female companionship." He said, "I did my best to accommodate as many women as I could—most of them through unprotected sex."[6]

Is AIDS primarily a homosexual disease? The reality of its spread in this country answers that question with a resounding *no*. It is spreading most rapidly today among intravenous drug users and their sexual partners—and among sexually promiscuous heterosexual young people.

Some predict that by the year 2000, AIDS won't even be remembered as a "gay disease." By then it will be known as a sexually transmitted disease among young people of all races. A study between 1985 and 1989 of more than one million teenage military recruits revealed that HIV infection is equally distributed between men and women.

The proportion of heterosexually transmitted AIDS cases among adolescents in the U.S. is twice that of adults. In New York City the rate is three times higher. While the number of heterosexual AIDS cases may still be small in terms of percentage, it is climbing rapidly. The number increased 40 percent between 1989 and 1990, more than any other category.[7]

Dr. Richard Grimes, an associate professor at the University of Texas School of Public Health in Houston, believes that America is already suffering from a full-blown heterosexual AIDS epidemic. He explained: "Lots of people in this country have multiple partners. This puts them and all their partners at risk." Grimes added that the epidemic is following a nearly identical course to that among homosexuals—it just began among hetero-sexuals a decade later.[8]

Unlike the U.S., in most other countries affected by the disease, heterosexual trans-mission is the rule, not the exception. According to the World Health Organization, 75 percent of infected people worldwide were infected heterosexually rather than homosexually.

The continent of Africa accounts for half of the world's estimated AIDS cases, and in more than eight out of ten cases there, the transmission was heterosexual. In Southern and Southeast Asia, where AIDS is spreading faster than anywhere else, heterosexual transmission is also more common.

William Hazlett, a physician studying and treating AIDS in Tanzania, says that virtually everyone knows about AIDS in Africa and how it spread, yet they ignore the danger. He says, "The lesson we have learned is that information is not synonymous with behavior change."

In the U.S., AIDS has devastated the poorer neighborhoods of New York City, Newark,

Baltimore, Washington, and Miami—cities where social problems and lack of good medical care are similar to those of Third World countries. But now "mini epidemics" are appearing in other areas, such as parts of Georgia and Texas.

Investigators suspect that AIDS patients who contract the disease in big cities tend to move back to their hometowns, either to be cared for by family members or to try and straighten out their lives. Once there, however, the victim may continue to be sexually active and become the source of a chain reaction of local AIDS infections, bringing the disease a little closer to home.[9]

A PERMANENT CHANGE OF LIFESTYLE

Once the HIV virus is discovered, the person's life can never be the same. It was while taking blood tests for a Los Angeles Lakers life insurance policy that Magic Johnson's infection was discovered. Johnson had just married his college sweetheart, Earletha "Cookie" Kelly, the previous September, and she was seven weeks pregnant. His first thoughts were of her and the baby, although tests on Cookie and their unborn child came up negative. (Their child, a son, was born safely in June, 1992.)

When he met reporters at the news conference in which he announced his retirement, Johnson vowed that his life was far from over. "I plan on living for a long time," he said. "I guess now I can enjoy some of the other sides of living."

The "other sides," according to Johnson, include continuing an intensive effort to educate young people about the dangers of a sexually promiscuous lifestyle. As he had influenced so many people with his status as a well-known athlete, he hoped to continue to influence them to learn the facts about AIDS for themselves and stop taking unnecessary risks by being sexually active.

Studies show that an alarming number of teenagers have the same attitude about AIDS that Magic Johnson had—the "It can't happen to me" attitude. It *can* and *has* happened to millions who right now may not even know they have contracted the disease.

Just after Johnson's announcement, *USA Today* reported that many teenagers responded positively to the news that one of their favorite sports heroes had AIDS:

- "Although this is a terrible thing to happen, maybe it will be a wake-up call," said Mike Cavaiola, 17, of Severna Park, Maryland. "This is a man making millions a year and, with all the money in the world, he isn't immune."

- Rob Bruce, 17, of Jacksonville, Florida, said: "To those who do have sex, it is an excellent warning. This just shows it can happen to anybody."

- "We have known about this disease for such a long time and it hasn't made a lot of difference. I hope kids will be more cautious. This is shocking and it is scary," said Claudine Ko of Irvine, California.[10]

After his shocking revelation had time to sink in, Johnson drew both criticism for his lifestyle and admiration for his honesty. Many felt he had set a bad example for his young admirers while others were pleased he hadn't tried to hide either his disease or the way he contracted it. Johnson said he just hoped to change people's attitudes toward AIDS.

Though he at first said he wanted to help educate the public about practicing safe sex, Johnson later stated on network television that the safest sex is no sex. "In God's eyes it was wrong . . . I was wrong. I wish it hadn't happened. . . . Now that I am battling for my life, I can only ask for forgiveness and ask people to educate the kids and help find a cure for AIDS. I'm telling kids—*no* sex is the safest sex."[11]

How could Earvin Johnson, a man who had everything—a beautiful fiancée, money, the adoration of millions of fans—ignore the danger of contracting a lethal disease? Johnson was raised by parents who stressed morality and Christian values, and he stated publicly that he knows "in God's eyes, it was wrong" to be sexually promiscuous. But like many other young people who "knew better," he made wrong choices which forever changed his life and the lives of those who love him.

Early Victims of Aids _____

You hear about the Magic Johnsons and other celebrities who are forced to deal with AIDS, but this killer epidemic is shattering the lives of *thousands* of other "unknown" families and individuals across America. Most of the people who live and die with this disease will never make the ten o'clock news or have their stories told in the local paper. And the few like Kimberly Bergalis, who become highly visible, will pay a high price for their fame.

As you can see, the HIV virus can be contracted in a number of different ways. Some get it as a consequence of their sexual behavior and others as completely innocent victims. Yet they all have one thing in common—no one wants to have AIDS. The result of the disease is suffering and death.

The first known celebrity to die of AIDS was Rock Hudson, a well-loved actor whose career spanned 37 years. Hudson kept his illness a secret for two years before he finally revealed that he had flown to Paris to be treated with the drug HPA-23 at the Pasteur Institute.

Hudson was the third biggest box office draw of the '60s, behind only Cary Grant and Elizabeth Taylor. In the '70s, he found renewed fame on the television series, "McMillan and Wife."

He was also heavily involved in a homosexual lifestyle, often indulging in drinking binges and frequenting gay bars in San Francisco. Columnists, press agents, friends, and colleagues shielded Hudson from publicity about his lifestyle. But though they could cover for him out of affection, no one could protect him from death by AIDS.[12]

Ryan White was another name in the news during the early onset of AIDS. He died April 8, 1990, at age 18, after leading a public battle against AIDS for five years. Life became complicated for this ordinary boy from Indiana when he was diagnosed with AIDS at age 13. His infection was the result of accidental contamination through blood transfusions that he needed for hemophilia, a blood disorder.

White made national headlines when he was expelled from school because of his disease. Anger and fear among teachers and parents about his presence raged out of control. After a shot was fired through his family's front window, they moved to another town.

He became a media personality, appearing on television programs, speaking at AIDS fundraising benefits, addressing national conventions and testifying before the President's Commission on AIDS. Yet White didn't enjoy the excessive attention. "It's embarrassing to be famous for being sick," he said. "I never wanted to be the AIDS boy who was always in the news. I just wanted to be like every other kid my age."

Ryan White died of recurring pneumonia which afflicts many AIDS patients. His doctor said his body was trying so hard to breathe that it finally just wore itself out.[13]

Actor Brad Davis battled AIDS in secrecy for six years before his death in 1991. "If an actor is even rumored to have HIV . . ." Davis wrote, "he does not work."

The 41-year-old Davis was best known for his role in the movie *Midnight Express*. His drug addiction was at its peak following the movie role, which led to his contracting AIDS in the '70s. "I was a total addict," he said, "a user of just about any drug I could get. And I was sexually very promiscuous." Davis left behind a wife of 15 years and an 8-year-old daughter who both tested negative for HIV.[14]

Is AIDS Preventable?

A gifted athlete, Magic Johnson, slept around and exposed himself to a disease that will surely end his life unless a cure is found during the next few years. A popular actor, Rock Hudson, frequented gay bars and practiced homosexuality while the specter of AIDS loomed. More recently another athlete, Arthur Ashe, the first black man to win the Wimbledon Tennis Tournament, also announced that he had tested HIV-positive. Like Ryan White, Ashe picked up the virus through a blood transfusion. While the disease claims some innocent victims along the way, there is much that can be done to prevent contracting AIDS.

Celebrities with AIDS become the topic of conversation in newsrooms, barrooms, locker rooms, and living rooms. You may have participated in some of these very discussions. But as you do, are you soaking up the facts about this disease as well? Are you applying what you hear to how you live your life? Each year thousands of teenagers become sexually active while those around them are dying of AIDS and suffering from other sexually transmitted diseases.

What I hope you will realize as you read this book is that every choice you make now can make a crucial difference in the outcome of the rest of your life. The Bible tells us, "Do not be deceived: God cannot be mocked. A man reaps what he sows" (Galatians 6:7).

Ten years ago, who would have believed there would be a disease as terrible as AIDS? So while the relationship "game" has changed for a lot of people, the rules of the game—the guidelines for living given by God in His Word— never change. God forgives sexual sin, yet the forgiven person must still deal with the consequences of his or her actions. And you may not be prepared to accept some of the consequences of being infected with the AIDS virus. Just one mistake could cost you your life.

———————◆———————

2

> *"Saying that the use of condoms is 'safe sex' is in fact playing Russian roulette. A lot of people will die in this dangerous game."*
>
> Dr. Theresa Crenshaw
> President's Commission on AIDS

The Deadly Facts About AIDS

J ENNIFER HAD BEEN ATTRACTED TO Ethan since the two of them had met in English class. One day she smiled at him across the room and that was all the encouragement he needed to ask her out. She flashed him a brilliant smile just before she said yes.

You might describe their mood as exhilarated and carefree as they left a Friday night party at a friend's house. The host's parents had been out of town and the alcohol was flowing freely. Ethan downed several beers with the guys and Jennifer helped a girlfriend finish off a bottle of wine. But neither of them would have considered themselves really *drunk*.

Jennifer was in the youth group at church, and Ethan had been attending as well, but they were getting tired of all the dos and don'ts they were expected to follow. After dating for a while, they had come close to having sex a few times, but so far they had stopped in time.

Tonight, however, when Ethan stopped the car on a dark road, things were different. They were no longer in control of their actions—alcohol had taken over. Almost before they knew what was happening, it was over.

Their pleasure had been short-lived, and now a more long-lasting guilt and fear took its place. Neither of them had planned to have sex. Jennifer kept thinking, *I wish I had waited*, and asking herself, *Will I get pregnant?*

Her fear quickly intensified into panic the next week when a speaker at their school assembly talked about AIDS and other sexually transmitted diseases. Jennifer suspected that Ethan had been with other girls before her, but she had no idea who they were or how many.

They discussed going to a local clinic for AIDS testing, but Jennifer was afraid of what they might find out. Besides, the guy at school had said it would be a month or so before they could know anything for sure. So they decided to wait and go for tests later.

Yet as soon as Jennifer determined she wasn't pregnant, she shoved the thought of AIDS to the back of her mind. Meanwhile, Ethan became interested in a new girl at school. And neither Ethan nor Jennifer ever made it to the clinic for testing.

SHORT-TERM AFFAIRS, LONG-TERM RISKS _____

Most of us like to think that the kind of "relationship" Ethan and Jennifer had doesn't happen very often, but we all know better. If something similar hasn't happened to you, then you probably have friends who found themselves in the same kind of situation. One or both of the people think the relationship is permanent, and they agree to have sex. But almost as soon as they do, the relationship disintegrates.

The emotional trauma of this kind of relationship is bad enough. Ethan and Jennifer "sowed" momentary pleasure and self-gratification and they "reaped" guilt, regret, and possibly worse. Their exhilaration and freedom felt great for a while, but had no lasting substance.

But in addition to the emotional and spiritual concerns of casual sex, today no one can afford to ignore the physical threat of AIDS. A brief relationship can drastically impact not only the two people who choose to become intimate, but also everyone involved with either of them in the future. It can even affect their children someday.

Pleading ignorance will not prevent someone from contracting AIDS. Each person must choose to be responsible for his or her own body and behavior. The responsibility lies with each of us as individuals—with you, because you are in danger of getting AIDS, even

from someone you trust and care about. And
you can pass it on to someone else.

You can avoid the likelihood of AIDS if
you make a commitment not to go along with
the crowd and experiment with sex and alcohol.
I would hope that such a commitment is based
on a personal relationship with Christ. Yet even
if that is not a basis for your decisions, you still
need to make a commitment to know the facts
about AIDS before you choose to engage in
sexual activity.

The fact that AIDS could actually *kill*
them had no effect on Ethan and Jennifer.
Even after they were informed of its dangers,
they acted irresponsibly.

How much do *you* know about the virus
that has become a matter of life or death for so
many young people? What are the facts about
the disease that has already killed more people
than two recent American wars? What is AIDS,
and how does it affect its victims?

A Scientific Look at AIDS _____

The following section contains a number
of medical and technical terms which provide a
scientific approach to the AIDS dilemma. Don't
be distracted by strange terms. Rather, be sure
to notice the *effects* of AIDS on the human body.

AIDS first came to medical attention in
1981 when homosexual men in New York City
and on the West coast starting dying from
diseases that had been seen only rarely and

almost never in men their age. Doctors eventually discovered a common virus, the *human immunodeficiency virus* (HIV) which causes AIDS.

The first AIDS report on June 5, 1981, identified five cases of a rare form of pneumonia. All five patients suffered a collapse of their immune systems along with a strange combination of opportunistic infections including *pneumocystis carinii pneumonia* (PCP).[1]

HIV often causes a brief, flu-like illness at the time of infection, but it can then remain dormant for years before showing any other symptoms. However, even if no symptoms of AIDS are present, HIV can still be spread to other people.

HIV affects the body's immune system, making it unable to fight infections and diseases. HIV is known to kill T4 cells, a critical component of the human immune system, by replicating, budding from them, and damaging the cell membrane. In simple terms, HIV actually becomes a part of your body's cells, hiding in them like a time bomb just waiting to explode. Without the help of the cells that make the body immune, diseases can move in without a fight.

It usually takes a period of several years before the virus develops into AIDS. People infected with HIV don't look like the pictures of AIDS patients you see in magazines and on television—they look and feel just like any normal, healthy person. They may not even know they are infected. That's what makes AIDS so deceptive and deadly—you can get it from someone who looks and feels as healthy as you do.

When the body's immune system has been severely damaged and symptoms begin to show, they vary from person to person. A condition called *AIDS-related complex* begins. Some people get fevers and diarrhea. Others have swelling in their glands and an oral infection called *thrush*. Many experience weight loss and an overpowering fatigue. Later, the victim will develop *opportunistic infections*, or malignancies which kill.[2]

Opportunistic infections are caused by agents already present in our bodies or our environment. They cause diseases only when there has been some sort of alteration in the person's cellular makeup. Some of them which commonly affect AIDS patients include:

- *Candidiasis:* A yeast-like infection that affects membranes, the skin, and internal organs. Inflamed white patches occur in the mouth, nailbeds, anus, esophagus, and the vaginal area. Internally, it can also affect the heart.

- *Cryptococcosis:* A fungal infection acquired through the respiratory tract. It affects mainly the lungs, but can spread to the kidneys and skin as well.

- *Cryptosporidiosis:* An infection caused by a parasite found in the intestines of animals. It can be acquired by some people through direct contact with infected animals. It lodges in the intestines and causes severe prolonged diarrhea that does not respond to most medications. It may be passed from person to person.

- *Cytomegalovirus* (CMV): A virus in the herpes family. It can be mild with no symptoms, or severe with aching, fever, sore throat, weakness, and enlarged lymph nodes.

- *Herpes simplex virus type I* (HSV-I) and *Herpes simplex virus type II* (HSV-II): HSV-I causes cold sores or fever blisters on the mouth or around the eyes. HSV-II causes painful sores on the anus or genitals.

- *Herpes zoster:* The same virus that causes chicken pox. It can lie dormant for years and reemerge as a localized infection of peripheral nerves (called *shingles*) and can lead to encephalitis.

- *Histoplasmosis:* An infection that may cause acute pneumonia or flu-like illness with inflammation of the joints.

- *Toxoplasmosis:* A chronic condition char- acterized by brain lesions.

Malignancies and other diseases seen in AIDS patients include:

- *Kaposi's sarcoma:* A tumor of the walls of the blood vessels that causes pink or purple lesions on the skin. It progresses rapidly in AIDS patients and causes death from major organ involvement.

- *Lymphoma:* A general term for growth of new tissue in the lymphatic system. Includes Hodgkin's disease, lympho-sarcoma, and malignant lymphoma.

- *Pneumocystis carinii pneumonia:* A lung infection that would normally be destroyed by a healthy immune system. It recurs in AIDS patients and becomes fatal.[3]

It goes without saying that AIDS victims suffer unbearably and some die tragic deaths. In addition to the physical pain, many also experience emotional separation from friends and family because they become ostracized. Some family members aren't able to come to grips with the horror of knowing someone they know and love is dying of AIDS. Hospital wards and AIDS hospices are full and sometimes cannot house the patients who desperately need their care.

How AIDS is Passed Along

How is HIV passed from person to person? This area of research has been hotly debated for some time. Some writers have claimed that

HIV can be transmitted casually—by coughing, from toilet seats, even mosquito bites.

Dr. John Dietrich, a Christian physician and infectious disease specialist who serves on *Focus on the Family's* physician advisory council, insists that there is no evidence to support such claims. Case studies and research of the virus show that it is transmitted by the exchange of body fluids such as blood, semen, or vaginal discharges. Most people get the AIDS virus by having sex or sharing drug needles with someone who already had it.[4]

Men with HIV can infect women as well as other men. Women can infect men or other women. Infected women can even pass the virus to their babies before and during birth and, in rare cases, by breastfeeding. More than a third of babies born to infected mothers will have the virus and develop AIDS.[5]

If you have questions about AIDS or how you might contract it, you are not alone. Below are answers to some of the most common questions being asked about AIDS. Most reliable health officials seem to agree on this information. I would like to reemphasize, however, that new discoveries about the spread of AIDS are being made almost daily.

(1) You cannot get AIDS from *giving* blood. Each needle is new and sterile. It is used only once, then destroyed.

(2) Since 1985, your chances of getting AIDS from *receiving* a blood transfusion are

very low. Donors are now screened and the blood is tested for the virus.

(3) Most researchers claim that, unlike many other viruses, HIV does not spread by traveling through the air. HIV is fragile and dies quickly outside the body. There are no documented cases of AIDS contracted from shaking hands, hugging, coughing, or sneezing, or from being passed to someone else by way of toilet seats, swimming pools, food, insects, animals, or eating utensils.

(4) Although the AIDS virus can be found in saliva, there hasn't yet been a documented case of AIDS spreading by that method. It is rapidly destroyed by digestive enzymes, so kissing is considered low-risk at the present.

(5) The easiest way of contracting the disease is through anal intercourse, which is widely practiced by homosexual men. Blood vessels rupture easily in the tissue that lines the anus and rectum, which gives HIV a direct passageway into the bloodstream.

(6) Though women are said to be more at risk than men during vaginal intercourse, men can contract the virus this way as well, especially if they have genital ulcers or breaks in the skin of the penis.

(7) Oral sex *is* considered a dangerous sexual activity because body fluids are exchanged.

(8) It is possible for the AIDS virus to be transmitted during contact sports such as boxing and football where bloody injuries occur.

(9) Condoms are *not* a sure way to protect against AIDS. They can come off during intercourse. They can break. And certain kinds allow the virus to pass through their porous membranes.

[Having listed this information, it should be noted that not *all* medical experts are in absolute agreement on every point. If you wish to pursue more information about the spread of AIDS, I would recommend a book by Dr. Lorraine Day, *AIDS: What the Government Isn't Telling You* (© 1991, Rockford Press, Palm Desert, CA). She documents cases that suggest AIDS may be more easily spread than most people now think (possibly through passionate kissing, for example).]

Within a month or two after the body acquires the HIV, it produces antibodies that a blood test can detect. If a person is tested too soon after being infected, the test may come back negative. So if you are planning to have a blood test, make sure it is conducted by a qualified healthcare professional who will be thorough and advise you of the facts about AIDS and testing procedures.[6]

The old saying, "An ounce of prevention is worth a pound of cure," has never been more true. Antiviral drugs such as AZT can slow the progress of HIV disease, and new treatments have made some AIDS-related infections more manageable. But *there is no known cure for AIDS*. It is always fatal.

OTHER SEXUALLY TRANSMITTED DISEASES _____

Magic Johnson was right on target when he said the safest sex is no sex. This truth was illustrated on a recent television program in which a young girl was being tested by her doctor for the AIDS virus. Her boyfriend had lied to her about his sexual history and about using a condom. She said, "You mean just because I spent ten minutes in the back seat of a car I now have to wait and worry for months, not knowing whether or not I have a disease that can kill me?" The doctor's reply: "I couldn't have said it better myself."

While AIDS is the most serious of the sexually transmitted diseases (STDs), it isn't the only one that can have devastating consequences. STDs are on the rise in the U.S., affecting twelve million Americans, including three million teenagers each year.[7]

Dr. Antonia Novello, Surgeon General of the United States, says that every 30 seconds in this country a young person contracts a venereal disease.[8] And according to the Centers for Disease Control, one in every 300 college students tests positive for HIV.[9]

Other STDs—like syphilis, gonorrhea, chlamydia, pelvic inflammatory disease, genital herpes, genital warts, and hepatitis B—can all be treated. Yet if they are not detected early they can cause serious illness, birth defects, and even death. Gonorrhea and chlamydia are leading causes of infertility. Untreated syphilis can ravage the heart and brain. The sexually transmitted viruses that cause hepatitis and genital warts also cause certain cancers. All are preventable and most are easily cured. But AIDS is not curable.[10]

Despite the grievous threat of AIDS and the risk posed by STDs, statistics show that young people are still making dangerous choices when it comes to sexual activity:

- In San Francisco, the HIV infection among teens is estimated to be doubling every 16 to 18 months.

- A Gallup poll taken just after Magic Johnson's shocking revelation shows that 32 percent of the people interviewed still weren't willing to limit the number of their sexual partners.[11]

- Fifty-seven percent said they weren't willing to have their blood tested to find out if they are carriers of the AIDS virus.

- *Seventeen* magazine reported that in 1991, 71 percent of girls ages 18–19 were sexually active, as compared to only 54 percent in 1984.[12]

- According to the national Survey of Family Growth, eight years ago only 19 percent of girls under 15 were sexually involved; today the number is nearly 50 percent higher, with 7 of every 10 teens having sex by age 18.

- One million teenage pregnancies were reported in 1990. Nine percent of girls become mothers before turning 18 and another nine percent have abortions.

- The Centers for Disease Control report that one in four sexually active teens will contract a venereal disease before completing high school.[13]

For many young people, the confusing journey to adulthood is frustrating enough without having to contend with the threat of a deadly disease. Romantic love, as they understand it, can cost them their lives.

Consider, for instance, a 17-year-old high school student named Carmen who had sex for the first time when she was 13. At one point she developed symptoms of venereal disease, but didn't seek treatment until a year later. She is now involved sexually with a teenage boy, and she believes everything he tells her. "Even if he was screwing around," she said, "nothing would happen because he says he'll never mess me up, and I believe him. We don't need a condom because he says he loves me."[14]

BLIND TO THE RISKS?

Other young people—perhaps even you or someone you know—are having their emotions manipulated in the same way. They believe whatever their partners tell them because their feelings have blinded them to the risks. Many are afraid to ask about a partner's sexual history or AIDS because they fear being rejected. Some teens don't understand the concept of being faithful to just one partner. Says one worker at a South Carolina student health service, "To them monogamy means you're sleeping with one person at a time."

One study among college students in Southern California found that nearly 50 percent of the men and 40 percent of the women said they would lie about how many other people they had slept with. One man in five said he would lie about having been tested for the AIDS virus.

And even with all the advertising and school programs that promote condom use during sex, that concept is not working. Sociologists at the University of California tell us, "the people most at risk are taking the least precautions." They found that less than 20 percent of the currently sexually active women and men reported using condoms 75 percent of the time or more. The behavior of sexual participants was not due to lack of information. Some had three or more sexual partners in three months, and they knew enough to be concerned about AIDS, but the facts didn't convince them to use condoms.[15]

Some secular and Christian leaders believe that the current campaign to get teenagers to use condoms as protection against AIDS and other diseases is really doing more harm than good. Many feel that the notion of safe sex is just a myth, including former Surgeon General Everett Koop. He has said: "The country has become involved in 'condom mania.' I don't feel particularly happy about the role I've played in that. Condoms are a last resort."[16]

According to a National Survey of Family Growth, the failure rate of condoms used by teenage girls to prevent pregnancy is 18.4 percent. And using condoms for protection against HIV is such a bad idea that another study, conducted by the federal government in the Los Angeles area, was stopped because participants were at too great a risk of contracting HIV.

Dr. Harold Jaffe, chief of epidemiology at the Centers for Disease Control in Atlanta, said: "You just can't tell people it's all right to do whatever you want so long as you wear a condom. It's just too dangerous a disease to say that."

Dr. Theresa Crenshaw, a member of the President's Commission on AIDS, feels even more strongly: "Saying that the use of condoms is 'safe sex' is in fact playing Russian roulette. A lot of people will die in this dangerous game."[17]

The AIDS dilemma rages on in our society, and yet sexual behavior—or misbehavior—hasn't changed much. In fact, it has steadily grown worse. AIDS education, safe sex campaigns, and scare tactics haven't worked. Kids are being enticed into lifestyles that seem glamorous and exciting—and they are dying as a result.

◆

3

"When I played football, we had specific rules by which we played. . . . There are certain rules about how to use sex. . . . There is no sex, no orgasm that any man has ever experienced that I know of that is worth dying for."

Miles McPherson
Former member, San Diego Chargers

All the Pleasure, None of the Guilt

Even though I am being candid, many rock lyrics are too disgusting and revolting to quote here, words that only a few years ago were seldom heard outside of the world's sleaziest dives and hellholes. Yet, young people and older are constantly bombarded with these litanies from hell—four-letter words and the like for the sex act, words for warped, twisted activities, words which humiliate and despise girls and women, words which spew hatred for good and weird adoration of all that is base, low, and downright dirty.

The "f word" is bandied about as commonly as "Hi" and "How are you?" It's strange. It's against the law in many places to pray, but there it's deemed OK to curse, talk filth, and take God's name in vain.

"Madonna was a sweaty pinup girl come to life. She wiggled her tummy and shook her a——. She smiled lasciviously and stuck out her tongue. She rolled around on the stage and got down on her knees in front of a guitarist. And when she raised her arms, her scanty see-through blouse also rose, revealing her purple brassiere. . . . What Madonna is really about is sex, and there was plenty of that."[1] Millions of young people view and hear videos and songs like these as regularly as they brush their teeth—blaring from car stereos, playing in their rooms at home, or spun by dance club disc jockeys.

If our music market is any indication, America is obsessed with sex. And today's musicians are cashing in on that obsession. If no one bought their music, they would be out of business. So they are simply giving people what they want—and then making hefty bank deposits.

Sexual overtones—if not graphic portrayals—permeate today's television programming, movies, advertising, books, and magazines. And of course it's not all aimed exclusively at teenagers—adults have sexual obsessions as well.

The sex obsession is everywhere. Even small children waiting in line with Mom at the supermarket are a captive audience for the bizarre tabloids and suggestive magazine covers.

It's a perfectly natural response for young people to be curious about something being thrown at them from every direction that looks hotter and more provocative than anything they've ever experienced. But when you think about AIDS and other sexually transmitted diseases—and hopefully you *will* think about them—remember that old expression, "Curiosity killed the cat."

SEX IN ADVERTISING

Television is a very persuasive medium that can educate in either a positive or a negative way. TV producers acknowledge that their commercials *can* influence the public by charging enormous fees for a 30-second commercial. Yet they then try to claim that the sex-and-violence-filled shows have *no* effect on the public at all. They can't have it both ways.

Since the early days of Madison Avenue advertising, sex has been used to manipulate people into buying a product. If an ad agency can get you to buy a pair of jeans, a six-pack of beer, a CD, a movie ticket, or anything else by means of a subliminal (or blatant) sexual tease, it has succeeded in two areas. First, the media pros have achieved their business objective and made the sale. But the by-product is something much more subtle, something orchestrated by Satan himself. The use of sex to sell products manipulates young people into missing the importance of an act God designed to be beautiful and fulfilling between two people who are committed to each other for life.

The most dangerous thing about this practice is the package. A commercial product is wrapped up in a glittering, glamorous, sensual box. The message is, "Just enjoy yourself. Don't think about anything but how good it's going to feel when you own and use this product."

One low calorie food product, at least, is honest with its message: "All the pleasure. None of the guilt." But most companies are much more subtle, implying that you can have casual sex without negative consequences. It's a lie, of course, but take a close look at the ads you see. Many would have you believe otherwise.

Sex on Television/Films _____

If television advertising seems heavy on sexual promises, the actual shows may be even worse. One reason programming portrays values contrary to what many parents want their children to learn is that most of the "media elite" are far more liberal than Americans in general. A 1986 media study done by Professors Rothman and Lichter at George Washington University found that "the people in decision-making positions are more likely to condone things like abortion, homosexuality, and extramarital affairs. They have far less faith in God, and two thirds admit that they are trying to bring about more of an 'anything goes,' godless society."[2]

We are exposed to hour after hour of television programs with role models who are deceitful, self-centered, materialistic, unethical, and immoral. Frequently disrespect is shown for authority figures, family, religion, and the sanctity of life.

Another problem is the unspoken message being sent to young men and women who can't compete with the glamorous and sexy images portrayed by handsome, muscle-bound actors and slim, beautiful actresses. The average young person's self-image is not that good to begin with. When such people measure themselves by the professional actors they see in television shows, movies, and videos, they are sure to find themselves lacking. The media undermine the self-esteem of young people by putting so much emphasis on sexuality, looks, and material possessions.

In 1990, about 20,000 sex scenes were shown on television, and 80 percent of all references to sexual intercourse were between characters who weren't married to each other. So young people receive a mixed and inconsistent message. On one hand they are bombarded with a system of entertainment and advertising that uses sex as its focal point. On the other hand they are being told by parents, teachers, and counselors: "Have 'safe sex.' Here's a condom. Or better yet, don't have sex at all. There's a killer disease out there." No wonder they're confused.

The American Academy of Pediatrics has found that children today spend more time watching television than they do in classrooms. They spend hours each day (on average) in front of the set, yet less than five minutes daily in meaningful conversations with adults. In many homes, television has become the baby-sitter and the educator, as well as the entertainer.[3]

Other studies show that children watch about three hours and twenty minutes of TV each day, teens about three hours and fourteen minutes.[4] According to *TV Guide*, 34 million people watch MTV each week. If you have ever watched this music channel, I think you will agree that much of its programming involves some sort of sexual activity or innuendo.

For those of us who live in the age of AIDS, the fare being offered on television is not just poor, but deceptive as well. Many are literally being lured to their deaths. The obsession with sex has formed a cocoon around kids that cushions them from reality—the realities of teen pregnancy, of sexually transmitted diseases, and of AIDS.

For some, the sexual behavior portrayed in the media initiates a personal obsession with sex that grows into an addiction that cannot be overcome without professional help. For a few, only the most vile kinds of pornography can satisfy their sexual cravings. In extreme cases, people act out what they see by victimizing others. One case in point was mass murderer Ted Bundy.

Writer Susan White of Knight Ridder newspapers thinks parents should be horrified by information their kids are getting from television. "Now that AIDS has entered the picture," she said, "what was once merely offensive borders on the dangerous because it ignores the death threat that lies hidden in television's free-for-all view of sex." She also said, "Even people who aren't particularly religious or conservative are beginning to say enough is enough."

White describes two specific examples. One is a quote from the TV sitcom, "Herman's Head," which featured an attractive young woman, offended at being called nice. "Nice is boring," she said. "What I am is six or seven hours of great sex."[5]

A second example was a Jordache commercial featuring a young woman in a slinky dress dancing to a rock song while the cameras zero in on strategic parts of her body. A handsome young man begins to dance and remove his shirt. The commercial ends with the woman pinned against a wall as the man rubs against her. There is no dialogue, but the message is clear: Sex for sale in the guise of blue jeans.

One of the most popular teenage television shows in recent years is "Beverly Hills 90210." The program portrays the lives and relationships of students at a Beverly Hills high school. One episode showed sex between a teenage couple, once in the young man's bedroom and again in the back of a limousine after a rock concert.

The couple eventually broke up because the young man realized the girl was dating him only for materialistic reasons. While the program did attempt to some extent to portray reality and create characters who show responsibility for their actions, there was no moral as far as sexual promiscuity was concerned.

In addition to the content of this particular episode, the promotional scenes for the following week showed the characters trying to deal with the issue of condoms in schools. And the advertising, naturally geared toward teenagers, featured lots of attractive, scantily clad girls.

It is no surprise that the sexual content in shows on cable channels is less restrictive than in network programming. Many homes, even those with small children, subscribe to cable. Here is a sample of what the cable schedule offered recently in just one week:

- *Night Shift* (Rated R)—Henry Winkler and Michael Keaton operate a prostitution ring out of a morgue.

- *Ski School* (Rated R for strong language and sexual situations)—Ski bums and bunnies on the slopes.

- *Wild Orchid* (Rated R for strong language and sexual situations)—Mickey Rourke as a voyeur bent on seducing a young lawyer.

Psychiatrist Melvin Anchell explains that a favorite argument given to justify showing actual sex scenes in today's movies is that people who are in love engage in sex. Therefore, producers say, they have an obligation to make their pictures realistic. But as Anchell points out, such an impression of realism is incorrect.

"Sex is an intimate affair," Anchell said. "Two normal people in love seek solitude during sexual relations. If movie producers portrayed sex realistically, they would show lovers on the screen becoming impotent when performing sex openly before an audience."[6]

James Weaver of the University of Kentucky found that portrayals of sex—not violence—lead viewers to lose respect for women and to trivialize violent acts like rape. He said men who watched sex scenes from even ordinary R-rated movies developed a loss of respect for women and believed women to be more promiscuous that they had prior to the viewings.

Professor Dolf Zillman of Indiana University says that married couples who watch sex scenes between consenting adults often become dissatisfied with each other. The men in particular see their wives as less attractive.[7]

Sex in Music

The AIDS epidemic hasn't affected the sexual messages promoted by many rock groups through their music, either, as evidenced by the lyrics at the beginning of this chapter.

The ever-popular Madonna, who for years has danced onstage in lacy lingerie and simulates sex acts with other dancers, is still producing videos that push the limits of sexual imagery. One of them, "Justify My Love," was so objectionable that even MTV refused to air it.

The fear of AIDS is hitting home in the behavior and music of some artists—but they still resent it. Metallica's lead singer, James Hetfield, says that some younger musicians are resentful that AIDS is keeping them from enjoying the free sex they believe is "part of their rock and roll heritage." Hetfield added that he sometimes wishes he could go back to the '70s when AIDS was nonexistent.[8]

Teenagers Respond

In February, 1992, ABC produced a news special hosted by Peter Jennings called "Growing Up in the Age of AIDS." The town-meeting audience format included lots of teenagers, parents, and medical experts. A toll-free phone line was open for calls from people across the country.

One caller from Texas expressed concern about sex in the media. He called it "the media bombardment of selling products with the use of sex—from beer to autos . . . even underwear." Jennings asked for response from teens in the audience. Here are some of their comments:

> "I think the media doesn't have any type of correlation between using sex as a way to sell things and having safe sex portrayed in that type of advertising. So yeah, it gives mixed messages. It's giving you the message that it's OK."

> "I feel the media's doing a terrible job portraying sex for the simple fact you see everybody doing it. That makes me want to do it 'cause I feel like—and I think teenagers feel that—it's the thing that's happening."

> "You see a beer commercial, you know, girls calling up to a guy in his room, and right away there's contact, but there's no relationship. And the media pushes stuff that is false. There are no ads on television for 'just say no' to premarital sex. Everyone's body is beautiful and precious, and if we begin to have respect for ourselves, maybe we'll say, 'Wait a second, there is a right way and there is a wrong way. Let me try to find the right way.' And that will help in this whole process of spreading AIDS."

Ohio teenagers were asked about their response to the previously mentioned suggestive Jordache commercial:

"Yeah, it gets you pumped up. You turn to MTV . . . then you see this girl in a tight dress, you know, and she's looking good. I mean, she is looking good."

"The way we see [sex] in TV and movies might [cause us to want] to do that, because everyone who does it in the movies looks like they're enjoying it, so . . ."

"Seven o'clock in the morning you'll find [sex], and one o'clock in the afternoon you'll find it. You can find all different kinds of channels on TV."

Jennings then asked for a show of hands from teenagers who felt television advertising emphasizes sex to the extreme to sell products. More than half the teens present raised their hands.

One young woman, Krista, who has AIDS, had this comment: "I'm here to tell you [getting AIDS] happens. You know [TV should] make it bad for once, make it happen the way it happens in the world. Then they can show it, but at least they wouldn't be glamorizing it and making it seem like nothing bad is ever going to happen to you if you [have sex]."[9]

In fact, bad things happen every day to kids who get involved in sexual relationships much too early—bad things like one million teen pregnancies a year (1990 figures) and

400,000 teen abortions per year in this country alone.[10]

But the commercials and videos don't show the morning after the party where someone had too much to drink and ended up sleeping with a stranger. They don't show the aftereffects of the one-night stands where a young woman feels used and degraded. But of course they wouldn't—guilt and shame don't sell products.

It seems the world is having one big party—a sex party. And you're invited. When: Anytime. Where: Anywhere and Everywhere. Have a great time!

If you accept this invitation and attend the big sex party, tragic results are inevitable. Contrary to what musicians, movie and television producers, and advertising executives would have you believe, there *are* consequences to promiscuous sex. This truth was expressed well by youth evangelist and former San Diego Charger, Miles McPherson.

He said: "When I played football, we had specific rules by which we played. If you broke those rules, you were penalized. There are certain rules about how to use sex. Sex is a beautiful thing; it's very enjoyable, but when you go outside of those rules, you have consequences. The consequence we're talking about today is dying. And there is no sex, no orgasm that any man has ever experienced that I know of that is worth dying for."[11]

Let me leave you with these thought-provoking lyrics from the rap group Salt-N-Pepa:

AIDS ain't got no smell or taste
It don't care about your race
You see a nice kind face, you think you're safe?
I'm sorry, that's just not the case.[12]

———————◆———————

4

"I thought my commitment to change would be my first step toward a new life of joy and happiness. But there was one major problem I hadn't expected: AIDS."

Jerry
A Christian AIDS victim
who died in 1988.

Why
Am I
So Empty?

J ERRY WASN'T A FAMOUS ATHLETE like Magic Johnson, or a movie idol like Rock Hudson. He was a church kid and an honor student. Eventually he had become a successful architect. He was someone's son, someone's brother.

Jerry was a Christian who led a homosexual lifestyle for seven years. On June 13, 1988, he died of AIDS.

The son of born-again, dedicated Christian parents, Jerry was involved in most church activities. He was a Royal Ambassador. He went to Vacation Bible School in the summer. He even learned to sing "Jesus Loves Me" in Spanish.

At age five—on the same night he accepted Christ—Jerry was sexually molested by an older boy at a church camp. He was too embarrassed and ashamed to tell anyone what had happened, but the incident would haunt him for many years to come.

That event, along with a move to a new city, a grandfather's suicide, and other family-related factors helped mold him into a self-conscious and angry adolescent. His anger was a mask for all the confusion and hurt he felt inside, yet he couldn't bring himself to ask for help.

He had lots of friends, though he never really allowed anyone to get too close. On the surface he looked like a typical teenage boy, but inside he struggled with the overwhelming fear that he was, or would become, gay. He hid his fear from everyone, not wanting others to know his terrible secret.

Jerry buried his insecurities by striving to achieve. He struggled for perfection in everything, even the way he looked. He was uncomfortable around girls, mainly because he feared their ridicule and rejection.

He began to drink, thinking that might ease his inner turmoil, but it only intensified his guilt and rebellious feelings toward his parents and their beliefs. Though he never lost his faith in God, he lost all respect for the church, especially after an unmarried male choir member made a sexual advance on a church outing. More and more, Jerry recognized the imperfections of Christians. His involvement with church was providing him more doubts than answers, and he wasn't sure he wanted any further part of it.

When he finished high school, a long list of honors and awards accompanied his yearbook photo, but he was still as confused as ever. He didn't consider himself a homosexual, yet he had no answers as to why he felt different, incomplete, and in need of something just beyond his grasp.

His college years were much the same as high school. He dated a beautiful girl for four years, maintained a 3.75 grade point average, and graduated with honors and a degree in architecture. He immediately joined President Nixon's Office of Emergency Preparedness, working for a while with the Housing and Urban Development's project for disaster relief. The job required him to move around the country to wherever he might be needed.

Despite his continuing doubts about the church, Jerry remained active wherever he was, walking a tightrope between his Christian beliefs and the confusion he felt. He even spoke on Layman's Sunday in a church in South Carolina, and taught a Sunday School class in Austin, Texas. Describing this time in his life, he said, "I looked great attending church and felt wonderfully spiritual teaching my class every Sunday. But that didn't matter because my heart was not pure in motive."

One night Jerry went to a gay bar in Austin with a young model he was dating. They went, he said, to this "fun place" to check out the classy art deco design. That was the beginning of his addiction to the homosexual lifestyle which held him captive for seven years.

"I took the 'homosexual drug' for the same reason others take chemical drugs," he said. "I wanted to feel better; I wanted to be accepted; and other things hadn't produced satisfaction."

After three years, Jerry was able to suspend his gay lifestyle for about a year, but then he slipped into it once again. He never abandoned his Christian involvements, at one point even traveling behind the Iron Curtain to smuggle Bibles to a missionary there.

Eventually Jerry moved from Austin to San Antonio, joining a group of developers to build an elite country club community. His move allowed him to leave behind the homosexual world he knew, this time for good. He immersed himself in long hours at work as head of the project, as well as in reading his Bible and going to church.

"I thought my commitment to change would be my first step toward a new life of joy and happiness," he said. "But there was one major problem I hadn't expected: AIDS."

During a hospital stay for treatment of pneumonia in 1985, Jerry learned he had AIDS. As he cried himself to sleep that night, his last thought was, *How will I tell my mother?*

In fact, he didn't tell her for another year and a half when he was hospitalized again with pneumonia. When he finally did, his parents hugged him to them and asked him to come home.

Jerry then developed esophageal ulcers which made swallowing anything—even liquids—agony. He was terrified that one would rupture, causing him to bleed to death, or that he would pass out from the pain and never wake up. Within two months, his weight dropped to less than 120 pounds. He survived another bout with pneumonia, but about a year later he died peacefully in his sleep.[1]

This is just one story of a Christian who had to live—and die—because of the consequences of sin. Thousands of other people face similar consequences right now, people who would give anything to go back and start all over again.

TRUTH . . . AND CONSEQUENCES _____

Sometimes people get second chances— like Amy who became pregnant during the summer before her senior year in high school.

Like Jerry, she had childhood hurts and resentments that eventually turned into rebellion against her Christian upbringing. Amy was also unhappy with the relationships she had with some of the kids in her youth group at church. She remembers thinking, *If this is Christianity, I don't want any part of it.*

Amy and Jason had been dating for six months, and they were friends before they became lovers. One of the reasons Amy liked

Jason so much was because he didn't try to take advantage of her. "It just happened," she said. "Because he wasn't trying to take something from me, I gave it freely. I knew he had hurts in his life [from his parents' divorce] and I wanted to make him feel better."

Much later, Amy discovered that sexual intimacy was her way of gaining the male acceptance she craved and didn't receive when she was younger and her dad had worked long hours. She admitted she didn't worry about the danger of AIDS before she had sex with Jason since it was the first time for them both. Yet AIDS is not the only potential consequence of sexual involvement.

Amy later suspected she might be pregnant, and went to Planned Parenthood for a test. She was shocked to learn the results were positive. Up until that moment, she hadn't really believed it could happen to her.

She was scared—both of being pregnant and of telling her parents. Amy considered abortion, but knew she wouldn't be able to go through with it. She finally told her parents. They reacted with shock, anger, and disappointment at first, but eventually were able to work through those feelings and support Amy. She knew they felt the way they did because they loved her so much.

She decided to transfer to another district that had an alternative school just for mothers-to-be. She had heard a lot about open adoption and decided she liked the idea. She would be able to choose her baby's parents and keep in touch with them.

She chose a Christian couple who had been trying to adopt a baby for six years. When little Lorna was born, Amy was able to spend time with her in the hospital and make a videotape of them together before she placed the baby with her adoptive parents in another state.

At times, Amy said, she had problems with guilt, thinking that she took the easy way out. But she has been able to put those doubts to rest. "I gave her the best that I could," said Amy. "I wanted her to have a father, and she wouldn't have had that with me."

Jerry's case of AIDS and Amy's pregnancy are not rare, isolated instances. They merely reflect what goes on in the lives of many young people—yes, even Christians. Everyone has a need to be loved in a special way—but some of us try to fulfill this need in the wrong ways.

IS SOMETHING MISSING? _____

These two stories are a lot like the puzzles that say, "What's wrong with this picture?" What was wrong in each case was that God's direction was missing.

Perhaps you feel there is something missing from *your* life. It could be the acceptance of friends or the respect and trust of your parents. Maybe, like Jerry and Amy, you are confused and empty because you have made mistakes.

Perhaps you are disappointed because others have let you down.

Whatever the problem, don't leave God out of the situation. He can show how *you* must take responsibility for your actions as you attempt to fill that emptiness.

The void you feel can't be filled with sex outside of marriage. It can't be filled with drugs, alcohol, CDs by the hottest new musical group, or the best designer jeans money can buy. Our fleshly, physical appetites cannot be satisfied. If you try, they just demand more and more until they ultimately destroy you.

But something else *will* fill the void in your life and stop the longing, the craving you have for that "something more" you just can't seem to find.

The basic problem is not physical, but spiritual. Each of us was created with a spirit that needs to relate to God in order to find true fulfillment. Yet the sinfulness of man through Adam separated us from God and left that need unfulfilled.

The good news is that God knows our needs, and He wants to restore the relationship that sin has destroyed. So God sent Jesus to take care of your sin because He loves you and wants to relate to you. He wants to join His Spirit—the Holy Spirit—with yours. "He who unites himself with the Lord is one with Him in spirit" (1 Corinthians 6:17).

When you welcome Jesus into your life and allow Him to control every aspect of your being, He will fulfill every need. You won't receive instant gratification. Rather, you will go through a growth process, and you will probably have to learn the difference between wants and needs. But God will never let you down. James 1:4 challenges us to, "Let endurance have its perfect result, that you may be perfect and complete, lacking in nothing." Lacking in nothing sounds pretty good, doesn't it?

I hope you have already responded to God's love by believing in Jesus as your Savior and inviting Him to come in and take charge of your mind, your will, your emotions, and your body. If not, please keep reading.

It is Christ's love for you that makes the consequences of sin so important. Think about it—would loving parents allow their child to make choice after dangerous choice without a system of correction to draw him or her back into the protection of the family? Wouldn't they instead correct the child, giving him a sense of responsibility and spurring him toward maturity?

"You are no longer a slave, but a son; and since you are a son, God has made you also an heir" (Galatians 4:7).

"Endure hardship as a discipline; God is treating you as sons. For what son is not disciplined by his father? If you are not disciplined (and everyone undergoes

discipline), then you are illegitimate children
and not true sons" (Hebrews 12:7–8).

That's what being a Christian means—
you become part of a loving family! It's a big
family, and just like your family at home,
everyone makes mistakes. But when you make
a mistake, isn't it much more preferable to
answer to someone who loves you rather than
become more deeply entangled with a world
where "it's every man for himself"?

Even though your loving Heavenly Father
will forgive anything you do wrong, you still
have to live with the consequences of your
actions. Any consequence of sexual sin can
affect you psychologically, spiritually, and
physically. Young people who have sex outside
marriage, illegitimate babies, abortions, or
sexual diseases often suffer from guilt and low
self-esteem. They are disillusioned with
relationships because of their failures. They
feel used, confused, and betrayed. Perhaps this
is one of the reasons the teen suicide rate has
doubled in this country during the last 20
years.[2]

WHO ARE YOU FOOLING? _____

If there is a lesson to be learned from the
stories of people like Magic Johnson, or like
Jerry, it is not that we should practice safe sex.
If anything, we should practice "sacred sex,"

refusing to sow the seeds of corruption and destruction in our lives and bodies.

> "The one who sows to please his sinful nature, from that nature will reap destruction; the one who sows to please the Spirit, from the Spirit will reap eternal life" (Galatians 6:8).

Believe it or not, God's instructions concerning sex are for your own good. Did you realize that when you commit sexual sin you are actually hurting yourself? You are beginning within yourself an unholy desire to get more and more involved in sex until you are in complete bondage to sin. Being trapped in immorality is not what God wants for us. Yet we must choose to avoid that trap.

> "Flee from sexual immorality. All other sins a man commits are outside his body, but he who sins sexually sins against his own body. Do you not know that your body is a temple of the Holy Spirit, who is in you, whom you have received from God? You are not your own; you were bought at a price. Therefore honor God with your body" (1 Corinthians 6:18–20).

Committing sexual sin yields the control of our lives and bodies to something or someone else. And be aware that God's Word also tells us that sexually immoral people, adulterers, and homosexuals will not inherit the kingdom of God (1 Corinthians 6:9–10).

Fornication (sex without marriage),
adultery, and homosexuality are all sexual sins.
They were problems in the Apostle Paul's day
when he wrote to the Corinthians, and they are
still problems. But today's society has tried to
remove all the guilt and shame associated with
these actions that God has forbidden.

Many Christian young people are sexually
active. Our enemy, Satan, has deceived them
into thinking no one else knows, or will ever
know. And they may be able to fool everyone—
for a while.

You can fool your parents, your friends,
and your youth pastor. But so what? You're
really not getting away with anything, since you
cannot fool God! There is nothing you can do to
escape the presence of a God who loves you and
is trying to restore you to His family.

"O Lord, you have searched me and you
know me. You know when I sit and when I
rise; you perceive my thoughts from afar.
You discern my going out and my lying
down; you are familiar with all my ways.
Before a word is on my tongue you know it
completely, O Lord" (Psalm 139:1–4).

Are you a little disturbed to see exactly
how well God knows you? Or is it a comforting
thought to realize that you'll never have to face
the temptations of a sinful world on your own
power? Your answer will probably depend on
the choices you are making. You can't have it
both ways. You can't ask for God's power and

wisdom most of the time, but then expect Him to look the other way while you occasionally participate in sexual sin.

No matter what sins you may have committed in the past or what consequences you may be facing right now, I encourage you to seek God. Simply ask Him for help as you would ask a friend or a parent, for that is what He is! He has already promised to help and forgive you (1 John 1:9).

Then find somebody who can help you deal with your situation in a practical way. If you can't talk to your parents, talk to *someone*— a school counselor, a pastor, a youth leader, or someone else who is mature and trustworthy.

Don't bear your burden alone. Satan likes nothing more than to see people isolated, withdrawn, and steeped in guilt. That gives him room to work on you, bringing doubt and confusion, and ultimately influencing you to make disastrous choices.

Nothing you have done—nothing—is beyond God's desire and ability to forgive. You have hope for a bright future in Jesus!

———————◆———————

5

> *"Neither do I condemn you. Go now and leave your life of sin."*
>
> Jesus
>
> (To a sexually promiscuous woman of His day)

Forgiveness: It's Why Jesus Died

I F YOU'VE EVER BEEN TO CHURCH, you've probably heard the word *forgiveness* a lot. But do you have a good idea of what true forgiveness is? How does it happen? Is it really possible for us to be forgiven—and to forgive others?

In the last chapter, you read about Jerry and Amy and the consequences each one faced because of sexual sin. In this chapter I want to tell you what they did about their situations. I want to talk to you about the forgiveness they found and how God showed them, in different ways, that sin can be forgiven.

This is the most important part of their stories. It's not a lot of fun to read (or write) about problems like AIDS, unwanted pregnancies, and other results of sinful behavior. Yet in spite of Amy's unexpected pregnancy—and even Jerry's tragic death—it was possible for each of them to overcome the despair of the situation and find a happy ending. The end of the story was the forgiveness each one experienced.

THE MIRACLE OF FORGIVENESS _____

The reason forgiveness is so important is because it's why Jesus died. For Jerry, forgiveness was not just possible. It was, in his words, a "miracle" that allowed him to die with peace and complete trust in God. Before his death, he said, "I knew that God hated homosexuality, but I also knew that He loved me and all the other homosexuals. I knew there was forgiveness for all of us. That God is always waiting to pick us up and dust us off is the miracle that made the most difference in my life."[1]

Why do Christians allow themselves to become involved in a homosexual lifestyle? Why do we hear so many stories today about prominent Christians who are involved in adulterous relationships and unethical behavior? Like Jerry, many of them are caught in a sin trap that they cannot seem to escape.

Sin can be exciting. It looks good and feels good—for a while. Jerry felt the powerful force of sin constantly pulling at him, convincing him to try to solve his problems the world's way instead of God's way. He refused to take God at His word, even though deep down he knew he was violating God's laws. The guilt he felt pushed him further and further into sin and kept him in a struggle to try and justify his lifestyle.

But God never gave up on Jerry—and He doesn't give up on us. His love for us will—if we choose to believe Him—eventually draw us back to Him and to the truth of His Word, just as it did Jerry. Before he died, Jerry received God's forgiveness—a full pardon, so to speak—and he renounced the double life he had been leading for years.

"The important thing to me," he said, "is that I'm not a homosexual now. I profess that homosexuality is a sin. It is not the way God intended for us to live on this earth. Nothing good can come out of it. What does come from it is total destruction of mind, body, spirit, and the ability to utilize God-given talents to accomplish great things for His glory."

Jerry also found total acceptance and the peace that comes with forgiveness. During one of his trips to the emergency room, wondering if he would leave the hospital alive, he asked God to take complete control of his life. He prayed for God's help and asked Him not to leave him alone. God answered in a dramatic way.

God's overwhelming peace carried Jerry through some of the worst moments of his life. He had a deadly infection. His blood count was dangerously low. One of the nurses told him they had done all they could. But Jerry knew that God was with him, all because he had confessed his sin and given God complete control of his life.

Recalling this period of his life, Jerry said, "Even though I had become a Christian long ago, it was in that emergency room that I finally left the driver's seat of my life. I told God that He had my body, mind, and soul. I was done, and I was played out. I asked Him to take over."

God did take over, and He filled the void Jerry had felt all his life. He forgave Jerry and gave him the gift of His grace.[2]

THE VALUE OF SUPPORTIVE FRIENDS _____

Amy, pregnant at 17, found forgiveness in Jesus, too. But God showed His love for her in a different way—through the acceptance and forgiveness she received from a special group of young people at a church she was attending.

Although they knew—as she knew—that her sexual behavior had been wrong and sinful, they did not condemn or reject her. In fact, when she confessed her situation to them during summer camp, they prayed for her, hugged her, and made a commitment to stand by her as she carried and gave birth to her baby.

"They never looked down on me. I needed spiritual support, and I found it there," she said. "The youth group gave me what I needed— a spiritual life, not a social club. They helped me relate to the Lord and know His will and do it."

Both of these stories depict the complete forgiveness that Jesus wants to give everyone—Christians and non-Christians alike.

Maybe you've been involved in a sexual relationship. Maybe you've had *many* sexual relationships. Perhaps you've had a homosexual liaison or committed some other sin the Bible talks about. If so, God wants to forgive you and show you the total acceptance and fulfillment that you crave.

You may say, "That's not possible. You just don't know what I've done." But it doesn't matter. Nothing is too big or too bad for God to forgive.

PUTTING AN END TO SIN

The Bible gives us a wonderful account about a woman who had been caught in the act of adultery (John 8:1–11). The scribes and the Pharisees (who were strict and hypocritical leaders of the church) brought her to Jesus. They wanted Him to condemn her for her sin, and perhaps even suggest that she be stoned to death as the law of Moses instructed.

But His response was not what the church leaders expected. Jesus said, "If any one of you is without sin, let him be the first to throw a stone at her" (v. 7). And after the Pharisees all had sheepishly walked away, Jesus said to the woman: "Neither do I condemn you. Go now and leave your life of sin" (v. 11).

To you, God may seem unreal or far away. Or your image of Him may be distorted. Some people envision Him sitting on a throne somewhere in the sky with a booming voice, flowing robes, and a long white beard. They believe He watches every move we make, eager for us to make a mistake so He can zap us with a lightning bolt!

But that's not who God is or what He is like. If you are going to know Him and relate to Him, you may need to change the way you think of Him. He is watching you and He is waiting—waiting patiently for the opportunity to show you how much He loves to extend grace to those who believe in Him.

How much does God love us? "God demonstrates His own love for us in this: While we were still sinners, Christ died for us" (Romans 5:8).

If you want to know what God is like, take a look at Jesus. He left heaven and came to earth to live as we live (with all the struggles and sufferings) so He could truly relate to us. And ultimately He died in our place so we could find forgiveness for our sins.

Even though Jesus never sinned, He felt all the same things we do. The Bible says, "We do not have a high priest [Jesus] who is unable to sympathize with our weaknesses, but we have one who has been tempted in every way, just as we are—yet was without sin" (Hebrews 4:15).

Jesus lived for 30 years before He began His public ministry. Don't you think, during all those years, He experienced a lot of the same things you and I do? And even after—especially after—He began traveling about, He must have felt like questioning His decision to obey the Father's will for Him. He healed people, fed the hungry, and did only good for other people, yet He was rejected, opposed, and questioned. Later He was denied, deserted, and betrayed by some of His closest friends. He was beaten, mocked, ridiculed, and even spat upon.

This abuse continued right up until His ultimate rejection—a death sentence where He was nailed to a cross and left to die between two thieves. Did you know that during this time Jesus actually took our sin—your sin—upon Himself? He actually became sin, so we could know God's forgiveness.

He took your guilt, pain, and shame upon Himself. All the sins you have committed and all the sins you will ever commit were atoned for on that day. Jesus became guilty of every sin the world has ever known. He became guilty of immorality, adultery, homosexuality, murder, and all the rest. Why? So we can escape an eternal hell and have eternal life with Him instead.

"Christ redeemed us from the curse of the law by becoming a curse for us" (Galatians 3:13).

"God made Him who had no sin to be sin for us, so that in Him we might become the righteousness of God" (2 Corinthians 5:21).

"Let us then approach the throne of grace with confidence, so that we may receive mercy and find grace to help us in our time of need" (Hebrews 4:16).

Every person is born with a selfish nature, one that makes us want to do things our own way, without God's help. We are told that *all* have sinned and fall short of the glory of God (Romans 3:23). So how can we find the perfection we need in order to relate to God? Certainly not by trying to be "good" or living up to a set of rules. The Bible says that our salvation from sin is a gift provided by God's grace—like the gift of peace Jerry received in the emergency room.

"It is by grace you have been saved, through faith—and this not from yourselves, it is the gift of God—not by works, so that no one can boast" (Ephesians 2:8–9).

OUT OF THE SIN CYCLE

Have you ever tried to be "good," only to fail over and over again? When that occurs, doesn't the guilt from not being able to live up to your standards (or your parents' standards, your pastor's standards, etc.) usually make you frustrated and discouraged? And don't you continue to sin in an attempt to try and find some sort of meaning or joy in life?

Everyone gets caught in that "sin cycle" to some degree. There *is* a way out of it. But the only way out is by receiving God's forgiveness. And if you want out and are ready to let God help you find an escape route, here's how to receive His forgiveness:

(1) Admit that your sin has separated you from the God who loves you.
(2) Turn away from your sin and give control of your life to God. This process is called repentance.
(3) Place your trust (believe) in the fact that Jesus died for you and rose from the grave in victory over sin and death. Then ask Him to forgive your sin and restore your good relationship with God.

Trusting Christ is more than mentally recognizing Him as the Son of God or having an emotional experience. You must receive Him as your Lord and Savior by faith.

Let's take another look at a passage we examined in the last chapter:

"Do you not know that the wicked will not inherit the kingdom of God? Do not be deceived: neither the sexually immoral nor idolaters nor adulterers nor male prostitutes nor homosexual offenders nor thieves nor the greedy nor drunkards nor slanderers

nor swindlers will inherit the kingdom of
God" (1 Corinthians 6:9–10).

That's a list of terrible sins. And we don't
have to look far to see these same things taking
place today. Yet Paul was confident of the
mercy and grace available to us in Jesus.
Immediately following his list, he says,

"And that is what some of you were. But you
were washed, you were sanctified, you were
justified in the name of the Lord Jesus Christ
and by the Spirit of our God" (1 Corinthians
6:11).

Through a relationship with Jesus, you
can be "washed," which means "purified" or
"cleansed." Take a look at some of the verses
that tell you more of what it means to be
washed:

- Isaiah 1:18—Though your sins may be like
  a scarlet stain, Jesus' blood makes them
  as white as snow.
- Ezekiel 36:25—God will completely cleanse
  you from anything that has made you
  unclean.
- Hebrews 10:14—We have been sanctified
  ("made holy" or "set apart") by Jesus' one
  offering—His own life.

When you put your trust in Jesus, in
addition to being washed and sanctified, you
are "justified," meaning "cleared of any

wrongdoing, vindicated." It is just as if you had
never sinned:

- Psalm 103:12—As far as the East is from
  the West, that is how far God has removed
  your sin from you.
- Romans 5:1—Having been justified by faith,
  we have peace with God through Jesus.
- Hebrews 10:17—Jesus will not keep an
  account of your forgiven sins.

The only way to break free of sin is to
realize just how thoroughly Jesus has forgiven
us. It's such a transformation that we are like
completely different people:

"If anyone is in Christ, he is a new creation;
the old has gone, the new has come!"
(2 Corinthians 5:17)

Know What You Are_____

The knowledge that you are a new creation
helps you want to act like one. You don't want
to sin. You want to do the things which please
the One who has made you whole and forgiven,
don't you?

This truth is illustrated by a story I once
heard Dudley Hall tell. It's about a dog named
Scratch. He was new to the kennel, just a
puppy in fact. But it seems that the head dog,
Gus, didn't have a clear picture of what the

situation really was. He told Scratch that he was a cat.

So Scratch did everything he could to act like a cat. He wanted to impress Gus and all the other dogs with how good he could be. He ate cat food even though it made him sick. He tried to climb trees and fell on his face.

Scratch got so depressed that he even thought about killing himself. But one day Dudley came along and told him he was a dog. Then his life suddenly made a lot of sense to him—he felt like a dog! He barked, did all the things dogs do, and he was happy.

Scratch's problem was that he just needed to know who he really was. When he discovered that secret, he was able to act like himself.

It's much the same with Christians. If you don't know that you are a "new creature," you will continue to act like your old self. You'll follow the crowd, go along with the world's programming, and never discover God's plan for your life.

And the solution is so simple: accept God's forgiveness. Accept the fact that He has made you completely new. Relax and just be who you are—a new creature made to bring glory to Him!

————◆————

6

"It is not a religion or a church to which you [need to make] a commitment, but rather a person. Your commitment is with a living Christ who loves you."

Rodney Gage
Author and speaker

Sex Was God's Idea

B Y NOW IT MAY BE HARD for you to think about the topic of sex without associating it with a lot of negative images: AIDS, sexually transmitted diseases, undesired pregnancies, abortion, or so forth. And frankly, any young person who decides to have sex with someone else needs to be aware of these possibilities.

But you need to know something else. Sex was God's idea, and it is one of the most special gifts He has ever given us.

Are you confused? If so, you are not alone. With all the emphasis the Bible puts on sexual sins and their consequences, perhaps you had come to the conclusion that God frowns on sex. Or, depending on whom you talk to, you may have been led to think that sex is either a despicable act or something a single teenager is expected to experiment with.

Like many other things, sex can have quite different consequences depending on the context in which it is used. Many people have a distorted view of what love and sex are all about. To some, it's an anything-goes lifestyle. To others, it seems dirty. When people don't acknowledge the Bible as a source of truth, they create any number of opinions and philosophies to justify their sexual behavior. So in today's society, you have every right to be confused about the subject of sex.

GUIDELINES FOR GOOD SEX_____

This chapter will present how God feels about sex as He has explained it to us in the Bible. Many people fail to realize that sex is God's gift to us. He wants us to enjoy it. While *unrestricted* sex can cause serious problems, sex in its proper context can bring a man and woman closer together than perhaps any other experience. The one restriction that God puts on sex is that He intends it to be a sacred trust to be enjoyed by a man and woman *in a marriage relationship.* Only then can a couple enjoy the intimacy of sex without the fear, guilt, or other consequences that have been discussed so far in this book.

The Book of Proverbs was written by King Solomon to advise his son (and it applies to daughters, too!) against sexual promiscuity. Among the other good advice it contains is this challenge:

"May you rejoice in the wife of your youth. . . .
May you ever be captivated by her love. Why be
captivated, my son, by an adulteress? Why
embrace the bosom of another man's wife?"
(Proverbs 5:18–20)

Solomon knew the dangers of *promiscuous* sex, but he was certainly in favor of sex
between husband and wife. For example, he
also wrote:

"You have stolen my heart, my sister, my
bride; you have stolen my heart with one
glance of your eyes, with one jewel of your
necklace. How delightful is your love, my
sister, my bride! How much more pleasing is
your love than wine" (Song of Songs 4:9–10).

Happiness and fulfillment in marriage is
God's perfect will for you as a Christian, as the
new creature He has made you. It is when sex
is misused, abused, and even perverted that it
has a negative effect, many times leaving scars
that will stay with you for a lifetime.

The desire for sex is a strong physical
drive. People take advantage of that drive to sell
products, seek acceptance, and try to find
emotional fulfillment; yet the Bible says that
our bodies were made for God, not for sex:

"Offer your bodies as living sacrifices, holy
and pleasing to God—this is your spiritual
act of worship. Do not conform any longer to
the pattern of this world, but be transformed

by the renewing of your mind. Then you will
be able to test and approve what God's will
is—His good, pleasing, and perfect will"
(Romans 12:1–2).

Fellowship with God is the only intimate
relationship that will give you the acceptance
and fulfillment you are searching for. You don't
have to conform to the way the world thinks
about sex—your mind can be renewed to see it
the way God does. Then you can walk in the
perfect will of God for your life.

When you accept Christ as Savior, the
Holy Spirit lives within you, and you become a
temple (or sanctuary) of the Spirit of God.

"Do you not know that your bodies are
members of Christ Himself? Shall I then take
the members of Christ and unite them with a
prostitute? Never! Do you not know that he
who unites himself with a prostitute is one
with her in body? For it is said, 'The two will
become one flesh.' But he who unites himself
with the Lord is one with Him in spirit"
(1 Corinthians 6:15–17).

When you are in Christ, you are alive to
God and dead to sin. You are provided with
wisdom and power from a resurrected, living
Christ! Jesus didn't just die for your sins—He
was *raised* from the dead, and now the Spirit of
God lives within each of His people. In fact, the
thing that distinguishes Christianity from every
other religion is that our Savior is still alive—

and living through those who have put their trust in Him!

When you have sex outside of marriage, you involve much more than just your body in the relationship. Your soul (mind, will, and emotions) and your spirit (the part of you that is indwelt by God's Spirit) is affected as well.

The reason premarital (or extramarital) sex is wrong is because a sexual relationship was designed to allow two people to become one. It is as intimate as two people can be. But the act of sex outside the commitment of marriage will never have the same positive effect. Instead, all sorts of "unholy unions" are created that leave scars of guilt and shame, emotional pain from failed relationships, and the ravages of disease.

God certainly doesn't want you to be miserable and torn apart by guilt and shame, or to suffer the physical consequences of sexual sin like AIDS and other STDs. The reason Jesus came into the world and died for our sins was so we could "have life, and have it to the full" (John 10:10).

The resurrection power of Jesus enables us to conquer sin and have victory over the scars of the past. And a personal relationship with Christ not only wipes out the sins of the past, but gives us victory in the future as well.

I believe the reason so many marriages end in divorce today (one out of two) is because large numbers of husbands and wives are dragging baggage from past sexual encounters into their marriage relationships. They have ignored God's instructions about sexual behavior, and then they don't know how to deal with the pain and frustration caused by their past actions.

But the simple solution is to first accept God's love and forgiveness. Then each person needs to commit his or her life—and body—to the Lord. I know, because it was no different for me than anyone else.

CONFESSIONS OF A PREACHER'S KID _____

Before I became a Christian, I had a tremendous void in my life that I couldn't seem to fill no matter what I did. I was raised in a Christian home. In fact, my father is a preacher.

As a preacher's kid, I wanted desperately to gain approval and acceptance from others. I was even willing to do things I later regretted.

I remember coming home Friday and Saturday nights after a night spent with friends. Often, I would take a shower and go to bed. But though I went to bed physically clean, I still felt dirty because of guilt and shame over my actions.

From my childhood, I did all the "right things" from a religious viewpoint—I went to church, walked down the aisle, and even got baptized at the age of six. Yet my life didn't seem to have meaning.

I had three older brothers whom I idolized as a kid. They all experienced the same struggle that I did during their teen years. (Thankfully, they all later put their faith in Christ, and their lives were changed completely.)

In spite of all my religious knowledge, I had no peace or purpose—that is until April 22, 1984. Two weeks before my high school graduation, I attended a revival in which my oldest brother, Daniel, was the evangelist.

As I listened to Daniel speak that night, I heard something that hit me right between the eyes. He said, "There is a difference between a 'head knowledge' of Jesus Christ and a 'heart knowledge.'"

At that moment God let me know the reason for the emptiness I felt—it was because I did not have a personal relationship with Jesus. Right then, I trusted Christ as my Savior. I can't even begin to explain the overwhelming joy and peace I found—and still have—because I gave Jesus control of my life.

Recently, my love for Him has grown even deeper. The reason? God answered a prayer I had prayed for a long, long time. He gave me the desire of my heart by bringing into my life a beautiful, godly woman who is now my wife.

On June 1, 1991, Michelle and I were married. And we are both very proud of the fact that neither of us had sex—with another person or with each other—before we were married. Michelle knew that God had someone very special with whom she would spend the rest of her life, so she waited for me—and I waited for her.

It is indescribable how exciting and fulfilling it is to know that neither of us had ever given our bodies to someone else, but rather saved the bond of sexual intimacy for each other. We both know now that this was God's perfect will and plan for our lives from the beginning.

DARE TO BE DIFFERENT _____

Sadly, studies show that Christian teenagers are not much different from non-Christians when it comes to sexual behavior. A recent survey taken by Josh McDowell's ministry showed that 43 percent of young people who attend church have sex by the time they are 18.[1] Christian parents and church involvement are no guarantee that a teen will choose to reject premarital sexual involvement.

Nevertheless, I want to tell you that you *can*, from this moment on, treat sex as the sacred trust God created it to be and save yourself for the person God will bring into your life. If you have already had sex with someone, claim the forgiveness that is available to you and let God wipe the slate clean.

But if you haven't yet decided to have sex with someone, I challenge you to wait. Don't take the risk of getting AIDS or some other venereal disease. Don't expose yourself to the consequences of sexual sin and perhaps carry the scars for years to come. One bad decision during a moment of weakness can affect everyone in your future—especially that very special person you decide to marry, and perhaps even your children.

A KEY TO SEXUAL PURITY _____

Waiting is something to be proud of, although some of your sexually active friends would have you to believe it is something to be embarrassed about. The four children of Richard and Renee Durfield have a unique story to tell about waiting for marriage. Kimberli is 25, Anna is 21, Timothy is 20, and Jonathan is 18.

The Durfield parents have developed a family tradition to help their children resist sexual temptation. It centers around what they call a "key talk." They set aside a special time to talk with each of their children about the need to make a commitment, or covenant, with God to save sex until marriage. At that time they give the child a ring shaped like a key (representing the key to his or her heart) as a reminder of the covenant the child has made with God.

During the "key talk," parents and child discuss the meaning of sexual purity, the biblical concept of making a covenant with God, and how important it is to remain pure. Then they pray together, and each child makes a covenant, with one parent as a witness, to remain a virgin until marriage. The rings are given as a reminder that, in whatever circumstances the child may be, God will give the grace to keep the promise.

The Durfields believe that a child's simple resolution to "behave" or follow a parent's set of rules won't be enough to provide him or her the strength to resist the kinds of temptations present today. It takes much more—the resurrection power of Jesus described previously in this book.

Today, more than ten years after her "key talk" with her mother, Kimberli says: "I especially remember Mom's telling me that night that sex was not our idea, but God's, so it had to be good."

Anna says that the covenant she made has strengthened her: "I've had strong sexual feelings and I still do. But because I've made a stand from day one not to have sex, I've been able to keep the covenant with God that I made the night of our key talk."

Her brother Timothy added: "I'm still tempted. But that ring on my finger reminds me of my covenant with God and the gift I'll someday give to my wife—a gift I've never given anybody else."[2]

Your family may not be anything like the Durfields. Your parents may have never given you a ring or anything else as a reminder to save sex for marriage. They may have never talked to you about sex. They may not even be Christians. But you can have a relationship with Christ that is just as meaningful and just as strong as anyone's who comes from a

Christian family. If you are serious about your commitment to God to stay sexually pure, He will help you. Willpower grows weak from time to time, but the indwelling power of the Holy Spirit never does.

THE NEXT STEP IS UP TO YOU

Perhaps you are like I was—a church attender who doesn't really know Jesus personally. Or maybe you don't go to church at all. Whoever you are, whatever your background, I invite you to receive Jesus as your personal Savior right now.

If you have seen yourself reflected in the stories or situations described in this book, if you realize that you need help or forgiveness, and if you believe Jesus took your place on the cross and died for your sin, then put your trust in Him. Here's a prayer you might begin with:

Lord, I know I have sinned. I know that I cannot make up for that sin by being good, by going to church, or doing anything to make myself acceptable in Your sight.

I realize that the blood of Jesus is the only way I can have a relationship with the God who created me. I know He has provided salvation for me as a free gift.

I receive that salvation right now. Thank You! I know that I have been completely cleansed and made whole. Help me to walk in that knowledge every day for the rest of my life. Amen.

Remember, it is not a religion or a church to which you have a made a commitment, but rather a person. Your commitment is with a living Christ who loves you and is concerned about (and involved in) every aspect of your life.

If you have already made a commitment to Jesus, you know you have a personal relationship with Him. But perhaps you need to to make a covenant with Him to stay sexually pure. If so, I invite you to pray this prayer:

> Lord, I realize that my body is Yours and that You live in me. I ask today for Your help in keeping myself sexually pure until marriage. Reveal Your truth to me in every situation and every relationship, so I can make choices that are pleasing to You and healthy for me.
>
> I promise to keep this covenant and to resist any temptation to break it. I ask You also to help my mate-to-be. Keep that person in Your love and protected from all temptation. In Your perfect time, bring us together in such a way that we will know we are meant for each other.
>
> Lord, I know You always keep Your promises. Help me to keep mine. Amen.

To close, I would like to leave you with a wonderful biblical promise: "Know therefore that the Lord your God is God; He is the faithful God, keeping His covenant of love to a thousand generations of those who love Him and keep His commands" (Deuteronomy 7:9).

Now trust God to lead you day by day, not only in making choices about sex, but in every situation. If you remain open to His direction, He will not fail you!

———————◆———————

Notes

Chapter 1

1. Bonnie Johnson, Meg Grant, Don Sider, *People* magazine.
2. "Growing Up in the Age of AIDS," ABC News, February 2, 1992.
3. Magic Johnson with Roy S. Johnson, "I'll Deal With It," *Sports Illustrated*, November 18, 1991, 19.
4. Moody Adams, "AIDS: You Just Think You're Safe."
5. Geoffrey Cowley with Mary Hager, "Sleeping With the Enemy," *Newsweek*, December 9, 1991, 58.
6. Magic Johnson with Roy S. Johnson, Ibid, 22.
7. John Eldredge, "The AIDS Scare, 10 Years Later," *Focus on the Family Citizen*, December 17, 1991, 7G.
8. Leslie Sowers, "Til AIDS Do Us Part," *The Houston Chronicle*, November 17, 1991, 7G.
9. Susan Okie, "AIDS Poses Catastrophe for Africa," *The Washington Post*.
10. "Magical Career Closes," *USA Today*, November 8, 1991, 2C–3C.
11. "Face-to-Face With Connie Chung," *CBS News Special*.
12. David Gelman with Michael Reese, "AIDS Strikes A Star," *Newsweek*, August 5, 1985, 68–69.
13. Ryan White and Marie Cunningham, "Ryan White: My Own Story," *Parents Magazine*, April 1991, 104–111, 208.
14. Tim Allis, Michael Alexander, and Samuel Mead, "When Midnight Comes," *People*, September 23, 1991.

Chapter 2

1. *Focus On the Family Citizen*, December 17, 1990, 12.
2. "HIV Infection and AIDS," The American National Red Cross, May 1989.

3. *Caring for Patients With HIV Infection,* Glaxo, Inc., 1989.
4. *Focus On the Family Citizen,* Ibid., 13.
5. *HIV Infection and AIDS,* The American National Red Cross, May 1989.
6. Ibid.
7. Geoffrey Cowley with Mary Hager, Ibid.
8. "Growing Up in the Age of AIDS," Ibid.
9. Tom Hess and Gentry W. Yeatman, M.D., "AIDS: The Despair Behind the Condom Craze," *Focus On the Family Citizen.*
10. Geoffrey Cowley with Mary Hager, Ibid.
11. Ibid., 53.
12. Curtis Pesmen, "Love and Sex in the '90s," *Seventeen,* November 1991, 63.
13. Patricia Freeman, "Risky Business," *People,* November 5, 1990, 50.
14. "Safer Sex," *Newsweek,* December 9, 1991, 52.
15. Ibid., 54–55.
16. Dinah Richard, Ph.D., "Has Sex Failed Our Teenagers?" *Focus on the Family,* 1990.
17. Tom Hess, "Safe Sex Hurts Kids' Health," *Focus on the Family Citizen,* May 20, 1991, 11.

Chapter 3

1. Michael Goldberg, "Madonna Seduces Seattle," *Rolling Stone,* May 23, 1985, 20.
2. "Important Facts Concerning How TV Affects Your Children," *Morality in Media,* New York, N.Y.
3. Ibid.
4. Ibid.
5. Susan White, "Television is Firing Blanks in War on AIDS," *Knight-Ridder News-papers,* Fort Worth Star-Telegram, January 13, 1992, 3E.
6. Melvin Anchell, M.D., "A Psychiatrist Looks At Pornography," Americans for Decency, Staten Island, N.Y.
7. "Research on the Effects of Pornography," Morality in Media, New York, N.Y.
8. Sharon Bernstein and Vincente Rodriguez, "Rock 'n' Roll in the Age of AIDS," *The Dallas Morning News,* January 12, 1992, 8C.

9. "Growing Up in the Age of AIDS," Ibid.
10. Paul Thigpen, "Safe Sex . . . Wait Until Marriage," *Charisma*, March 1992, 25.
11. *Growing Up in the Age of AIDS*, Ibid.
12. Ibid.

Chapter 4
1. Jerry Arterburn with Steve Arterburn, *How Do I tell My Mother?*, Atlanta: Oliver-Nelson Books, 1988, 23, 79, 85, 107, 183.
2. Paul Thigpen, "Safe Sex . . . Wait Until Marriage," *Charisma*, March 1992, 25.

Chapter 5
1. Jerry Arterburn with Steve Arterburn, Ibid., 102.
2. Ibid., 103, 114.

Chapter 6
1. Paul Thigpen, Ibid., 20.
2. Ibid., 22–23.